Terms and Conditions

LEGAL NOTICE

The Publisher has strived to be as accurate and complete as possible in the creation of this report, notwithstanding the fact that he does not warrant or represent at any time that the contents within are accurate due to the rapidly changing nature of the Internet.

While all attempts have been made to verify information provided in this publication, the Publisher assumes no responsibility for errors, omissions, or contrary interpretation of the subject matter herein. Any perceived slights of specific persons, peoples, or organizations are unintentional.

In practical advice books, like anything else in life, there are no guarantees of income made. Readers are cautioned to reply on their own judgment about their individual circumstances to act accordingly.

This book is not intended for use as a source of legal, business, accounting or financial advice. All readers are advised to seek services of competent professionals in legal, business, accounting and finance fields.

You are encouraged to print this book for easy reading.

Table Of Contents

Foreword

Chapter 1:
Introduction

Chapter 2:
Pinterest Basic Use Tips

Chapter 3:
Link Up With Trusted Bloggers

Chapter 4:
Don't Be Pushy, Be Unique

Chapter 5:
Provide Helpful Info

Chapter 6:
Get Creative

Chapter 7:
Make Your Product Users The Star

Chapter 8:
Choosing The Right Pictures

Chapter 9:
Update Frequently

Wrapping Up

Watch Your Etiquette

Foreword

Pinterest can be a great way to spread awareness of your business and its products. Many people use this social networking site for business and non-business uses. However, before jumping in to Pinterest to market your business, you may want to consider some of the following steps.

Pinterest Perfection
How To Use Pinterest To Monetize Pictures

Chapter 1:
Introduction

Synopsis

Pinterest is a social networking site that allows users to create virtual multimedia pin boards that they can share with other users. If you find a video that is appealing or an image that has captured your interest and you think that it is also relevant to your contacts' interests, then posting it on Pinterest is a great way for you to instantly share these images and videos with them.

Using Pinterest For Your Business

The great thing about Pinterest is that you can categorize the kinds of pin boards that you create based on your interests. You can also make use of its "Bookmarklet" application which allows you to directly pin an image or video that you find on the internet and it will be exported to your Pinterest pin board.

Although Pinterest was initially used for personal purposes, it has been found to be an efficient way to attract potential customers and may even help increase the Google ranking of a business. Thus, if you have a home business website and you want to gain more followings, Pinterest is definitely one of the creative ways that you can drive more people and generate traffic to your business site.

Pinterest And Internet Business Marketing

There are several aspects that make Pinterest relevant to your Internet marketing endeavors. When you are marketing your business, you want to be known under a certain type of brand. With Pinterest, you can create your very own branding and secure a reputation in your social profile based on the type of content that you choose to "pin" in your board. Your business will gain faster recognition if they can associate you with images that reflect your business and your brand.

Another aspect that makes Pinterest a good business marketing tool would be its link building features. When you "pin" and "repin" an image or a video, it creates a link which will direct your visitors to the original source. You can use this feature by pinning images from your own business site. This way, every interested user will be directed to your website once they click on your pin board. At the same time, when a person "repins" your images, it can be considered as a form of social referral. In today's society where social media dictates a person's decision to purchase a product or avail of a service, being socially endorsed by your contacts increases your chances of gaining new potential clients. All of these actions can create a cycle which in turn can help increase your website's traffic. This can potentially increase your Google search rankings as well. Just think of how all of these procedures can improve the visibility of your company.

Optimize Your Pinterest Profile

Pinterest can be quite addictive because it's too convenient to "pin" and "repin" images and share them with your contacts. However, since you are maintaining your profile for your business site, make sure that whatever you post on your pin board is actually relevant and reflects your business. You can optimize the use of your Pinterest by treating it as yet another business profile in social media.

Make sure to use a professional profile image and provide a short introduction about you and your business. Provide information on your Pinterest profile by talking about your business site, what products and services you offer as well as the kind of pin boards that your contacts can expect from you. Don't forget to include a link to your Facebook business page and business website. If you have received awards or additional credentials, mention them in your account information as well.

Invest The Time To Build Your Network

Networking in social media sites requires time. You can't create a profile, leave it as it is and expect to drive thousands of visitors to your website the next day. You need to set-up a professional-looking Pinterest profile and be consistent in providing relevant content every day. Know which users are good influencers in Pinterest and see which of your pins might be interesting to them. This will help you capture more attention. At the same time, make sure that your "pins" have quality and value in them.

See to it that your posts are relevant to your target market and don't pin images just because you want to sell your business. People go to social networking sites to interact virtually so they want to see something that is of great value to them.

Chapter 2:
Pinterest Basic Use Tips

Synopsis

Pinterest is a new interesting social site where you can share your interests in the most creative way. It is true that pictures can really say it all as you express thoughts with images. That is why more people are signing up in this unique website because of its features. If you are one of the people who are thinking to join, here are the basic facts about Pinterest.

All About Pinterest

Pinterest can be defined as it is - 'pin your interest.' It is a site where you can pin the images or even videos that interest you and share it to your online friends. You will also get to have your own profile page with all the pinned images or videos in it. You can even categorize them into albums to better organize your thoughts. To begin, just visit Pinterest.com and request fo invitation or ask one of your online friends to invite you.

Searchable Pins

Now, as you start making pins, you will definitely want it to be viewed by your online friends. The descriptions of your pictures may be as simple as 'funny!' or 'beautiful' but that does not really appear at the top when people use the search engine. Instead, you can use keyword descriptions to make it more searchable. With that, there is a higher chance that your pins will get repined. Pins can also be a way for you to grow your business. Make it one of your marketing strategies and see your sales go up!

Editing Pins

There are times when we mistakenly put a specific image or video to wrong albums. This is one of the common errors by users but it is easy to edit them. What you can do is hover your pointer to a specific image and choose the "Edit" option. You can then transfer your image or video to wherever album it should be in.

If you need to search for that particular image, just go back to you profile by clicking your name at the upper right part of the screen. Now, click the 'Pins' options where it leads you to all your pinned images from recent to older ones. If you already organized your images, then your 'Boards' will appear. With that, you can search your pins and organize them further.

Tagging By The Rules

If you want a specific person to view your image, tag their name into it. To do this, just add the '@' sign upon writing the description of your pin. It is also good to understand the rules of pinning and repining. This unique social media site is free of charge, so it is ideal not to abuse it by following the rules.

These are the basic things that you may want to know about Pinterest. The popularity of this social media site is growing as the days progress and you may find it interesting and unique especially when you love checking out pictures and videos. It can also be a good way to grow your business too!

Chapter 3:
Link Up With Trusted Bloggers

Synopsis

Pinterest has the power to open doors to numerous linking opportunities with the most popular bloggers in your niche. However, those doors can only be opened with the right keys and that's where your pins and boards come in.

Find Trusted Bloggers

Linking to just any blogger work well at all because that can actually drag down your online "credibility". Linking is about being seen with the right people – bloggers whom your market already trust or won't hesitate to trust. Basically, the best bloggers that you should aim to link up with are characterized by the following:

•	Has an active blog with a trusted domain, consistent high-quality traffic, and content that is relevant to your own business or blog

•	Has a strong social networking presence, preferably in Pinterest as well

•	Has a reputation for promoting only products or services that are truly of value to its target market

Building A Relationship With Bloggers Through Pinterest

Pinterest – just like blogging – can pave the way to building a relationship between you and the bloggers you like, respect, and would love to exchange links with. Most of the things that you do in blog marketing will also apply in Pinterest.

•	Post comments only when you have something unique, relevant, and of value to say.

- Share resources that may be helpful to the other blogger – even if they are not actually your own. A helping hand will always be appreciated!

- Only link to the blogger's post if it is truly relevant to your content and can serve as an additional value-rich resource for your own readers and followers.

The tips above will get you noticed, but it's unlikely that they will be enough to provide you with high-quality links in Pinterest. For a trusted blogger to actually link up with you, the next thing to do is to come up with a photo that he or she will be interested in enough to repin.

Now, remember that the most popular bloggers are in the position to turn you down. After all, there are dozens or even hundreds of other marketers who want the same as you do: a chance to link up to them. Your photos will only stand out among the rest if they can offer any – or even all – of the following.

- Creative images that ooze with personality
- Complex figures made easy to understand with infographics
- Illustrations containing numbered lists or bulleted points
- Original photos of your own and which you would want them to be one of the "first" people to repin

Pins are only one half of the equation, though. For the most popular and trusted bloggers to consider you a worthwhile partner for link exchange, they'll want to make sure that you are not simply a one-pin wonder. As such, it's also important to establish your own credentials before approaching them.

- Do you use your own domain for your website and/or blog?
- Are you active in social media?
- Do you update your Pinterest account frequently?

If you answer 'yes' to all of the above then you are well on your way to linking up with the most successful bloggers in your niche!

Chapter 4:
Don't Be Pushy, Be Unique

Synopsis

As an entrepreneur, you might have heard how Pinterest can help you attract potential customers by creatively developing boards that reflect your business and your brand. Indeed, Pinterest is becoming a venue for entrepreneurs to introduce their products and services through visual images instead of marketing through words alone.

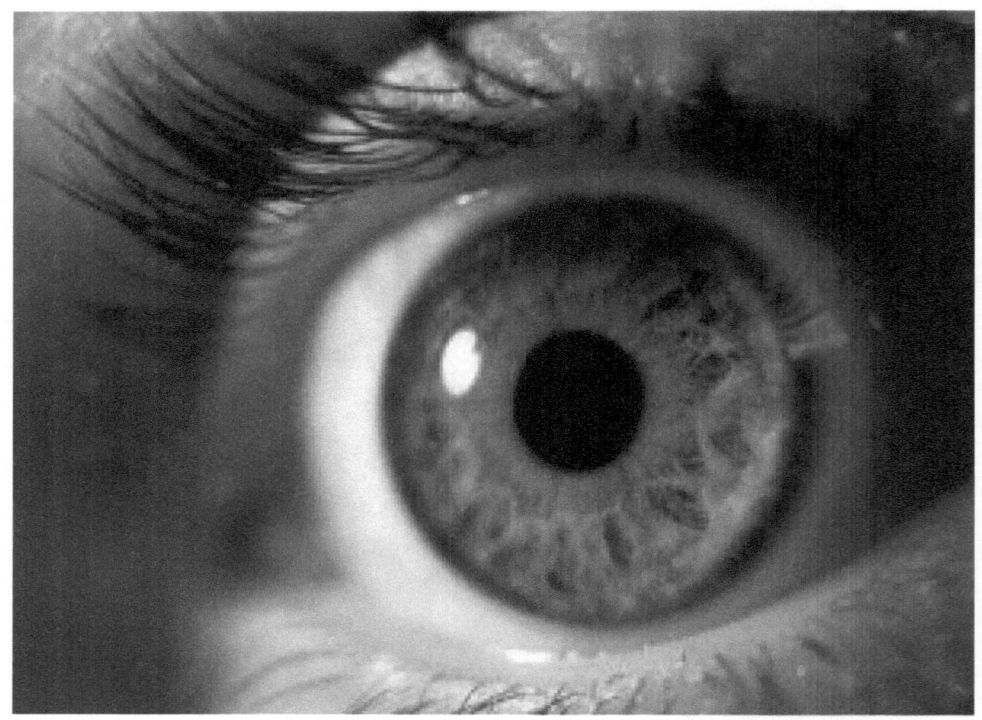

Examine It Well

In fact, you can find numerous sources on the Internet which detail how you can get the most number of "repins" by pinning it during the hours where your clientele are most likely on their Pinterests accounts, too. Although all of these tips are undeniably relevant in your goals of driving more visitors to your site, it might also be helpful if you actually take one step back and understand what Pinterest is actually about.

If you want to attract people without them thinking that you're a hard sell, stop being pushy with your business. Marketing your business is actually the same as marketing yourself as a person. You don't want to seem like you're trying too hard as you'd want people to be interested in you as you are. Be creatively unique and see which of your posts can actually capture their interest and be worthy enough to get a "pin."

Integrate not Separate

Don't obsess over your Pinterest as the be-all and end-all of your internet marketing efforts. Pinterest should serve as one of the venues where you can develop your brand creatively. Make your brand more recognizable by collecting images that are interesting and relevant to your consumers and to your business. You would want to curate the kind of content that will attract your followers mainly because they feel that your images speaks to them.

Diversify your content, make it exciting and be consistent with your updates. In addition, integrate your Pinterest account with your business profile on Facebook, Twitter and your business website to ensure maximum social media visibility.

Pin Content That Is Reflective Of Your Business

The rules of quality blogging also apply in Pinterest- don't post content just for the sake of having it. Your pin boards should be reflective of your company. You can capture the attention of pinners while trying not to oversell your products.

For example, the Humane Society of New York understands that the Internet loves anything adorable and cute. So they created a pin board full of adorable animals which are up for adoption. The company Benjamin Moore, on the other hand, makes use of small details in showing how their paints can make otherwise mundane things become more interesting. Thus, they posted quirky and colorful doors which they know Pinners will love to check-out.

You can even go slightly off topic with your posts. When you create your brand, you don't necessarily have to be too obvious. Sometimes, your clients will be reminded of your business through other images that are closely related to yours.

Adding a human touch to your Pinterest board will make you seem more interesting to other pinners. It will make them see that you are actually interested in providing entertaining and endearing content to them rather than just being bent on making a sale.

Of course, once you attract their interests, this is where you can start ushering them to find out more about you. Nobody ever likes to be with someone pushy, be it in a physical or an online setting. Be that person in a crowd who everybody wants to know more about.

Chapter 5:
Provide Helpful Info

Synopsis

Pinterest is not just letting your photos speak a thousand words. If you want to achieve your marketing goals with Pinterest, then you need to make sure that everything on your page – and not just your pins and boards – are speaking the right words in the language that your target market speaks.

Getting It Together

This part is where you upload a photo for your account and provide a short description about yourself or your company. Professional headshots are a must if you are marketing your authority in your niche. However, logos may be better to use if you want people to remember and focus on the products or services you're offering. Either way, it's important to make very good use of the limited amount of description space you get for your Pinterest profile.

Be concise as you explain who you are or what your company is about and what makes your products or services unique and better than the rest. Lastly, remember to write about your achievements.

The Boards

People are more likely to follow you on Pinterest if they can see that you have a very active page. This is where a little bit of visual strategizing will come in handy. To start with, you need to come up with 20 to 25 boards to make your Pinterest page appear bursting with information. Each board should have a minimum of eight to ten pins but we will go over that more later.

For now, focus on building your board list. All of your boards must of course be relevant to what you are offering but other than that they must be completely distinct from each other. They must represent different themes and all those themes must consequently be relevant and interesting to your target market.

Lastly, a Mashable study shows that Pinterest users pay most attention to the top two rows on a profile page. If you have a board that currently has the most vital information to share, that's where it should be placed in your page!

Pinning Outside The Box

Food should have nothing at all to do with your Pinterest account if you are an online accounting business…or should it? If you want to maximize the marketing potential of Pinterest, your answer should be yes.

Including pins and boards that focus on niche topics that have nothing at all to do with your business is important. There's a chance that you don't get to reach your customers through your usual boards and pins simply because they're unaware that your company exists or they're not even aware that they have a need for your products or services.

By targeting popular Pinterest niches like travel, beauty, food, or lifestyle, you get to enjoy a wider market reach. Your pins alone can convert Pinterest users into actual customers but you need to grab their attention first!

Obviously, uploading high-quality pins is the first way to do it. Secondly, you need to provide helpful information about your pin that is relevant to your business at the same time. Take as much time as you need coming up with pins and descriptions. Your efforts will be rewarded!

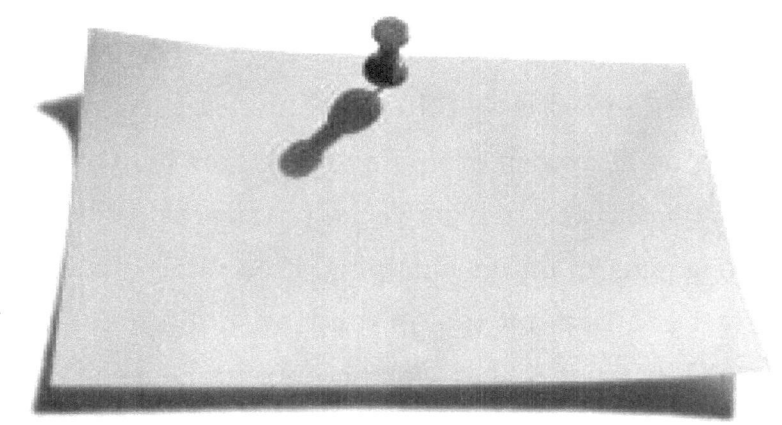

Chapter 6:
Get Creative

Synopsis

There is no denying that Pinterest is becoming one of the hottest social networking sites today. Aside from pinners that use the site to merely look for inspirations, more and more entrepreneurs are seeing the advantages of creating an account on Pinterest as well.

Another interesting fact is that 80% of Pinterest users are women and they have attracted women clientele through the help of the website's premise on creating and sharing visual pin boards. With the majority of women engaging in online shopping, it becomes a well-known fact that Pinterest is a relevant tool in drawing in more business clients. And this truth is what makes women entrepreneurs maximize what the site has to offer.

Women entrepreneurs have found out that the biggest draw on what makes Pinterest attractive is its capacity to let pinners get creative in developing their pin boards, whether it is about products that are sold online or services that they offer in the real world. If you want to monetize your images and gain potential clients to your business, read on and see how the power of creativity can help you achieve these goals.

Pinterest Provides Inspirations

There is something inspiring in seeing images and videos, knowing that they can work for you, too. This is exactly how event management companies make use of Pinterest. They organize boards which will help them translate their ideas into images.

Brides and other clients can take a look at their sample color schemes, wedding gowns, or events set-up. Some event management entrepreneurs even encourage their clients to create their own Pinterest accounts so they can pin images on their boards.

Aside from getting inspired, it is also a fun and easy way to collate images that the clients want without having to bring a bulky binder during their meetings. In addition, it makes it more convenient for both sides to share pin boards, especially if the client is from another location and cant meet-up physically. Aside from posting content directly from the business site, women entrepreneurs found out that they can actually post images which are indirectly related to their products and still get repins and recognition for it.

Run A Contest Through Pinterest

Nothing gets the interest of Internet users than a dose of healthy competition. You can run a contest which may be related to the product or service that you are offering in your company. Running a contest, in general, is a good marketing strategy and you can definitely incorporate this in your Pinterest.

You can ask pinners to create pin boards which they think are relevant to the theme that you have. You can then hold a contest where the pin board with the most number of pins and repins wins prizes. You can also use Pinterest as a way to advertise any upcoming onsite event that you are currently organizing. Whatever your strategy is, the visual imagery can draw in people to participate in your event. In addition, you can acquire more followers after holding such contests.

Use Pinterest To Introduce Your New Products Or Events

Since Pinterest relies heavily on images and videos, why not use it as a way to provide teasers for other pinners to see? Some television networks have already used this strategy where they pin photos of their news anchors doing funny acts backstage.

For your business, you can pin images of small details of what your new product will be without exactly giving it away. You can also give a sneak peak of an event that you are working on. The images that you will show can rouse the interest of pinners enough for them to excitedly wait for what you have in store for them.

Chapter 7:
Make Your Product Users The Star

Synopsis

As with any kind of business, it is important that you make your clients feel that they are your priority. This is applicable not only in providing excellent customer service but also when you are marketing your products and services. When it comes to internet business marketing, you also have to make your product users the star of your promotional campaigns.

With the advertising strategies that you have in mind, it can be quite overwhelming as you try to promote one product after another. But this shouldn't be the case. Especially when it comes to using social media marketing where you have the opportunity to interact with your clients and potential customers, it can be quite beneficial for your business if your customers feel that you have their interests as your top priority. So how can you integrate this aspect with social media sites such as Pinterest?

Know What Captivates Them The Most

People are visual creatures and thus, it is actually easy for you to determine the kind of things that your target market is mostly interested in. This is highly relevant when it comes to creating pin boards on Pinterest. Prior to posting images that you think will say a lot about your company, make sure that you are also aware of what they are actually interested in.

For example, the company Sony studied what their customers would most likely pin in relation to the company. They found out diverse interests ranging from Sony advertisements, logos, videos, and images of their products which were not exactly from Sony but are heavily related to the company.

This research led to months of creating pin boards which the company feels are visually appealing to their clientele. Most of their content at this time were repins of what other pinners had already shared on their boards.

Diversify Content

Although images can be visually appealing, they can also lead to loss of interest, especially if you see the same things over and over again. In addition, you wouldn't want your clientele to feel that they are constantly bombarded with marketing images, making them think that you've created your Pinterest solely because you want to sell products.

Make your pin boards interesting by mixing promotional images with fun multimedia. You can even create boards which encourage interaction among your clientele. For example, Sony developed a board known as "Rooms We'd Love to Live In," which features Sony products as well as interesting mixes of interior designs. This appealed to those who are into visually-appealing rooms but feel that they are not techie enough to be involved in Sony-related conversations.

Another interesting thing that you can do is to develop original images with concepts that are related to your brand. Have a shoot with artists who can make use of your products, company logo or other things that can be related to your business and offer pinners images that they won't be able to find anywhere else.

Make Things Easier And Accessible For Your Clients

Integrate your Pinterest profile with your other social media accounts. Make your website Pinterest-friendly so that visitors can easily pin content from your website directly to their pin boards by using a Pin-It plugin. See to it that your pin boards are also linked back to your business website. Promote your website as well with your Pinterest profile in other channels.

At the end of the day, you will realize that the way to make your product users the star would be to consider their interests and make it apparent to them. However, you will also find that they will continue to patronize your company because they actually want your products and services. But the best way for them to get at that point would be to entice them first.

Chapter 8:

Choosing The Right Pictures

Synopsis

A pretty photo does not always make a pretty pin. Consider that as a little bit of Yoda's wisdom for Internet marketers and bloggers wanting to make better use of Pinterest.

And as with all of Yoda's words, that one is true, too. What looks good right now on your laptop or mobile phone will not automatically look good as a pin. You need to consider numerous factors in order to truly determine which of the photos you want to use for marketing your business are truly "pin-worthy".

Size

Size definitely matters in this case – especially where profile pictures are concerned. Here are a few guidelines you are better off adhering to when uploading a profile picture.

- Keep it square. Personally crop or resize your photos if you have to because you do not want Pinterest doing it for you – and they will.

- Keep dimensions at 160 x 160 pixels. Again, it's better to do this on your own than let Pinterest do it for you. They won't care if they accidentally crop off your head in what's supposed to be a headshot.

- The subject should make up a large part of the photo. It must be visible and identifiable even when your profile photo shows up the size of a thumbnail.

Emotion And Information

It's not enough for your photos to be pretty. A picture that makes you 'ooh' and 'aah' will not necessarily motivate you enough to share it with other users or - in this case – repin it to your boards. In Pinterest, there are only two kinds of photos that matter.

- Emotionally-driven photos – These are the photos that make you laugh or teary-eyed. Sometimes, they may even be terrifying. Ultimately, these photos make people care about the message they're trying to promote, enough to 'like' or 'repin' it – or maybe even visit the link accompanying the photo.

- Information-driven photos – Info graphics make up some of the hottest photos in Pinterest. These photos are something that you're better off creating on your own, though. Just remember NOT to bore your readers with too many details!

Overbranding

Branding is still an essential and powerful marketing tool even in Pinterest, but you need to be careful about not overdoing it. Don't flood your photos with your company's name or logo to the point that your target market will be sick of seeing it. Worse, they might think you are being overly aggressive and that all you care about is making money instead of caring about their needs as prospective customers.

Rather than taking all sorts of creative snapshots of your brand logo, focus instead on pictures that show how your products or services are actually and presently being used in real life. Share and pin photos of customers with big smiles on their faces upon getting one of your products! Show it being featured in a trade fair.

Pictures will always speak louder than words so trust your photos to do their jobs instead of screaming 'buy me' at your customers with excessive use of logos.

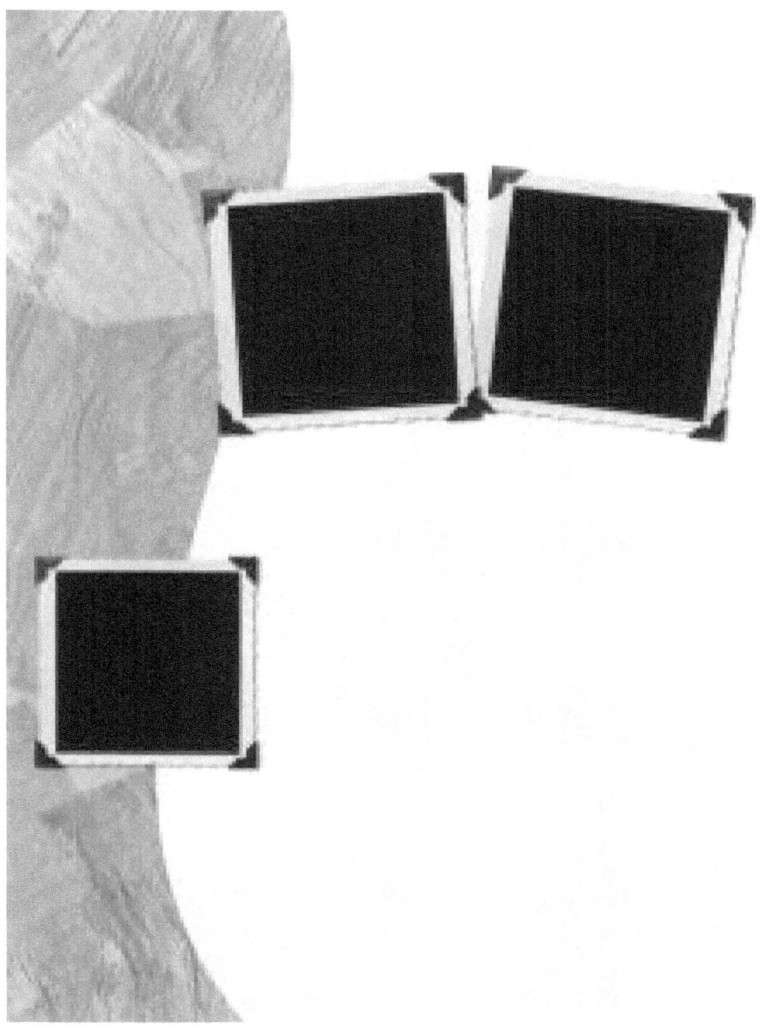

Chapter 9:
Update Frequently

Synopsis

When it comes to updating your Pinterest account, frequency is probably what you are worried most about. While it's true that frequency is a critical success factor for your marketing plan, it's not the only factor that you have to worry about.

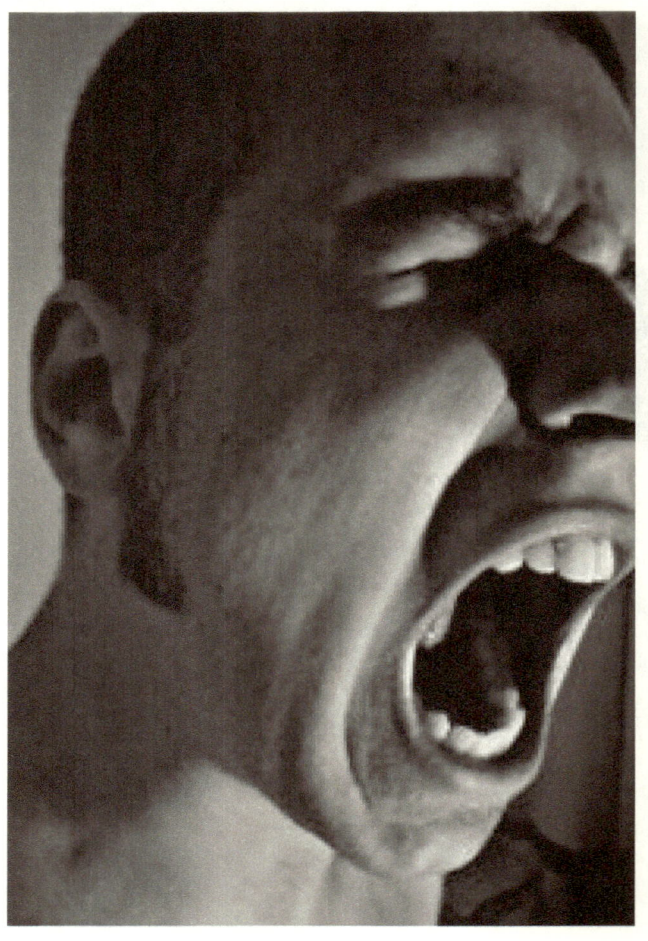

Frequency

Let's start by getting this out of the way since some of you may already have too much on your plate – marketing-wise. In Pinterest, the most active users get the most followers. At the very least, you need to come up with several new pins and repins every week.

Just one or two pins and repins for the week can be sufficient, but people will be expecting a lot of quality and value from those photos! Conversely, never sacrifice quality for quantity. If you are truly unable to come up with at least one original pin or photo for the week, you can always make do with two wonderful repins. Don't force yourself to come up with info graphics just for the sake of doing so. That's more likely to backfire than help you gain followers!

Consistency

Pinterest marketing is a lot like blogging. You need to come up with a schedule for your followers to depend on. Be sure to stick to that schedule because people will feel disappointed if they come visiting your page expecting new photos – and they find none. In the worst case scenario, you don't just lose a follower – you lose a loyal customer, too!

Timing

It's all about having the right photos showing up at the right time and place. Boards will take care of the latter, but you'll need to know more about your followers' online habits for perfect timing. What time in the day do they spend browsing pins? What time are they most likely to be free from distraction and able to fully focus on your pins?

Necessity

If you are just starting out, a weekly upload or pin will not be enough at all. You need to work overtime during the first few days and get your Pinterest page bursting in the seams and appear jam packed with relevant and interesting information and stories to share through your pins and repins.

Ultimately, it's about necessity. Be extra aware of what's going around you and pin or repin more photos if the situation calls for it.

Take the holidays for example. Christmas typically demands a higher output because this is the time where people are in the mood to buy. You need to take advantage of that and increased activity in Pinterest will surely increase your chances of capturing your market's attention.

JUST PIN IT!

To paraphrase the famous slogan of a sport company, that's all you really have to do in the end. If you came up with a photo worth pinning or you found a photo worth sharing – just pin it! Forget all about the timing or the schedules. It's just as important to be the first to pin a photo in Pinterest so if you have the chance to enjoy that – just pin it!

Wrapping Up
Watch Your Etiquette

The popularity of the social media site Pinterest is vastly increasing. In fact, since its inception in 2010, it is now considered as the third most popular social networking website after Facebook and Twitter. The premise of Pinterest relies heavily on creating visual boards that pinners can pin and repin.

Although it initially captured the attention of pinners for personal use, it is undeniable that it is now considered as one of the most influential sites for business entrepreneurs who aim to gain better social media visibility. Even if there are no rules on how you operate within your Pinterest account (except of course if it is offensive), there are certain unspoken rules that you have to observe to ensure that you are within the bounds of Pinterest etiquette. As an entrepreneur, failure to observe such can actually hurt your following.

Give Credit where it is Due

This applies to almost all things and it works on Pinterest as well. Since you probably won't be posting original content every single time, make sure to give credit to the original source. This is highly ethical and it complies with the Pinterest guidelines as well.

At the same time, don't directly pin an image just because you saw it on Google and you liked it. Chances are, you will be able to find the original source by clicking on the image or the link. Make sure to provide information on the name or website where you got your source. You also wouldn't want to see your photograph or your works online without being credited, do you?

Be Organized

Pinners will follow boards that interest them. Thus, if you have a board about "Bedroom Ideas", your followers expect to see images of bedrooms and not images of cute puppies, no matter how adorable they can get. Organization is the key to making sure that you hold the interests of your followers. If you want to have a repository of random images, you can do so, but categorize it accordingly.

Don't Spam (Intentionally Or Otherwise)

It may not be your aim to spam pinned images but at the same time, it is hard to believe that you can find more than twenty images to pin and repin within an hour. Select only those which you think are really relevant to your pin board, especially if you are running a Pinterest account which is linked to your business website.

It will be hard for you to advertise your business through images if your followers are starting to feel that your "pins" are seemingly irrelevant to their interests. They might even start to ask why they're following you.

Put A Bit Of Effort Into What You Post

Say you saw an inspiring image that you think speaks volume about your company. Pin it and then don't forget to add a label to it. You may place a short description telling why you pin the image or you may just say something on what the image is all about. When it comes to putting an effort into your pins, see to it that your posts are visually engaging and appealing. Avoid pinning images that are too small or too big for your followers to appreciate. Also, don't post images which are too pixilated to even recognize.

Following these tips will actually take less than a fragment of your time. When you watch your etiquette in social networking sites such as Pinterest, followers will be more engaged to see what you have in store for them. They may even be curious enough to click your images that will direct them to your business website or repin your post so that their contacts can see it as well.

www.ingramcontent.com/pod-product-compliance
Lightning Source LLC
Chambersburg PA
CBHW030542220526
45463CB00007B/2945